A Gift from the
Lammie Williams Fund

RYE FREE READING ROOM
Escape to the Library

HOW ARE THEY DIFFERENT?

Tell Me the DIFFERENCE Between a

BEE and a WASP

Leigh Rockwood

PowerKiDS
press
New York

Published in 2013 by The Rosen Publishing Group, Inc.
29 East 21st Street, New York, NY 10010

First Edition

Editor: Joanne Randolph
Book Design: Kate Laczynski

Photo Credits: Cover (bee) Sergey Lavrentev/Shutterstock.com; Cover (wasp), p. 14 Elliotte Rusty Harold/ Shutterstock.com; p. 4 nespyxel/Flickr Open/Getty Images; pp. 5, 11, 17 (right) iStockphoto/Thinkstock; p. 6 Maggee/Shutterstock.com; p. 7 Kletr/Shutterstock.com;p. 8 Kim Taylor/Dorling Kindersley/Getty Images; p. 9 Nicolas Reusens/Flickr/Getty Images; p. 10 Media Tuerto/Flickr/Getty Images; p. 12 irin-k/Shutterstock.com; p. 13 Alexsmaga/Shutterstock.com; p. 15 Ron Rowan Photography/Shutterstock.com; p. 16 Bill Beatty/Visuals Unlimited/Getty Images; p. 17 (left) Daniel Prudek/Shutterstock.com; p. 18 juanjofotos/Flickr/Getty Images; p. 19 (left) xtrekx/Shutterstock.com; p. 19 (right) Smit/Shutterstock.com; p. 20 Photo Researchers/Getty Images; p. 21 Adrian Roth/Shutterstock.com; p. 22 Ariel Bravy/Shutterstock.com.

Library of Congress Cataloging-in-Publication Data

Rockwood, Leigh.
 Tell me the difference between a bee and a wasp / by Leigh Rockwood. — 1st ed.
   p. cm. — (How are they different?)
Includes index.
ISBN 978-1-4488-9639-4 (library binding) — ISBN 978-1-4488-9736-0 (pbk.) — ISBN 978-1-4488-9737-7 (6-pack)
1. Bees—Juvenile literature. 2. Wasps—Juvenile literature. I. Title.
QL565.2.R636 2013
595.79'9—dc23

                                    2012022551

Manufactured in the United States of America

CPSIA Compliance Information: Batch #W13PK5: For Further Information contact Rosen Publishing, New York, New York at 1-800-237-9932

CONTENTS

LET'S LOOK AT BEES AND WASPS

Bees and wasps are both insects known for their stings. It can be hard to tell them apart without looking closely. Scientists group these animals into a suborder called Apocrita. A suborder is a group within an order that has a lot in common. Believe it or not, ants are

Bees tend to have rounder bodies than do wasps.

Do you see how this wasp has a narrower body and a more clearly defined waist than the bee on the facing page does?

among the thousands of **species** that belong to this suborder, too.

Bees and wasps share many physical characteristics and some behaviors, but each type of animal has qualities that set it apart. This book will show you how to tell the difference between the two insects.

WHEN A FAMILY IS A SUPERFAMILY

Beekeepers keep hives of honeybees so they can collect honey, beeswax, and other products. They also may rent out their colonies to help pollinate farm crops.

Bees and wasps belong to an order with many different species. For this reason, scientists further break down the Apocrita suborder into several superfamilies. A superfamily is a group of scientific families within an order or suborder that has a lot in common. Apoidea contains all of the more than 16,000 bee species and many kinds of wasps.

Another superfamily called Vespoidea contains another group of roughly 5,000 wasp species. Among the species in this group are wasps commonly known as paper wasps, hornets, and yellow jackets. With so many members, it is no wonder that it is hard to tell bees and wasps apart!

Have you ever seen bees buzzing around your food at a picnic? Those are likely not bees, at all. They are yellow jackets looking for meat or sweet things to bring back to the nest.

HOW ARE BEES AND WASPS ALIKE?

Bees and wasps share a similar body plan. As do other insects, they have bodies that are divided into three parts. First there is the head, which has two **antennae** and **compound eyes**. Behind the head is the **thorax**, where two sets of wings and six legs are attached.

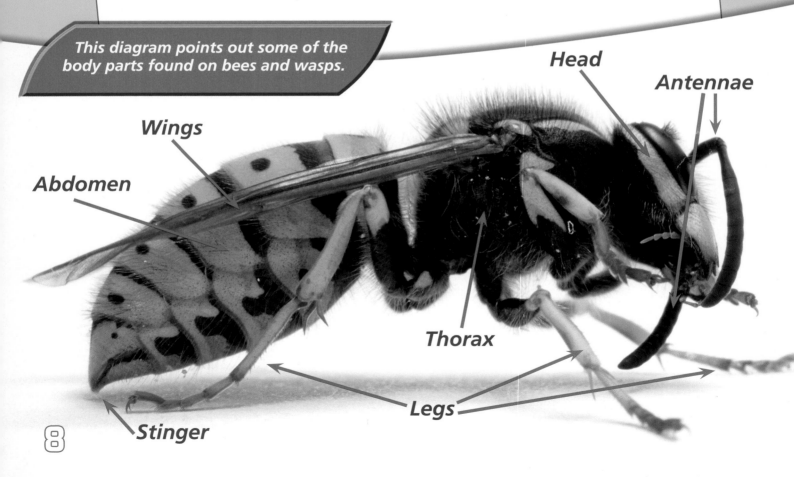

This diagram points out some of the body parts found on bees and wasps.

Head

Antennae

Wings

Abdomen

Thorax

Legs

Stinger

Bees and wasps both have large compound eyes. The black parts coming from this bee's head are the antennae.

In both animals, the thorax narrows into a waist, where it meets the **abdomen**. The abdomen is where the dreaded stinger is found on both bees and wasps.

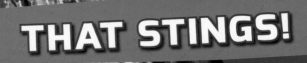

THAT STINGS!

This bumblebee has a curved smooth stinger.

Both bees and wasps are known for their stings, which deliver a dose of **venom**. Only females have stingers, though. Bees use their stingers only for **defense**. Wasps are more **aggressive** stingers. They will more readily sting for defense, and some species also sting **prey**.

You may have heard that bees can sting only once. This is true only of honeybees. These bees have stingers with more barbs than other wasps and bees have. This means that when a honeybee stings, the barbed stinger gets stuck in the skin. As the honeybee tries to pull the stinger out, part of its body rips off, killing it. Other bees' and wasps' smooth stingers can sting more than once.

You may wonder why only females have stingers. This is because the stinger develops from what would have been a female's egg-laying parts.

COMPARING BEES

SCIENTIFIC SUPERFAMILY	Apoidea
APPROXIMATE NUMBER OF SPECIES	16,000
STINGER	Females only
STINGS FOR	Defense
DIET	Herbivore (pollen)
HOME	Hive
BODY SHAPE	Round body with waist
BENEFITS TO HUMANS	Pollinate flowers, provide honey and beeswax

and **WASPS**

Vespoidea	*SCIENTIFIC SUPERFAMILY*
5,000	*APPROXIMATE NUMBER OF SPECIES*
Females only	*STINGER*
Defense and some species sting prey	*STINGS FOR*
Omnivore	*DIET*
Nest	*HOME*
Narrower body, more defined waist	*BODY SHAPE*
Kill pest insects, some species help pollinate flowers	*BENEFITS TO HUMANS*

BUZZING BODIES

Although bees and wasps share a body plan, there are differences in the ways their bodies are shaped. Wasps' abdomens have a more pointed shape while a bee's is more rounded. Additionally, the point at which a wasp's thorax and abdomen meet is much

This bee has a metallic green head and thorax. It is a kind of sweat bee that makes its home in Florida.

This wasp is mostly black, with small bands of white. Its wings are shiny and blue. You can see that it has a narrower body than the bee on the facing page.

thinner, giving it the look of a more slender waist between the two body sections.

You are likely most familiar with the yellow and black stripes that bumblebees, honeybees, and many wasps have. Bees and wasps come in lots of other colors, though. For example, orchid bees, which live in tropical South America, can be **iridescent** shades of blue or green!

Bees often have special parts on their legs called pollen baskets, which they use to collect lots of pollen. Do you see the large yellow circle of pollen on this bee's legs? That is the pollen basket full of pollen.

Another way that bees and wasps differ is in their diets. Bees are **herbivores**. They eat only pollen and nectar from plants. They have long, tubelike mouthparts called proboscises that they use to drink nectar. Bees usually have hairy bodies or hairy legs, which they use for collecting pollen.

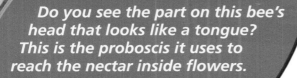

Do you see the part on this bee's head that looks like a tongue? This is the proboscis it uses to reach the nectar inside flowers.

Wasps often eat insects. Some wasps will lay their eggs in an insect's body. When their babies hatch, they have a ready-made meal!

Wasps often prey on other insects or spiders, which they kill using their stingers. They have mandibles, or jaws, instead of proboscises, for eating their prey. Some wasps eat nectar, too, but all wasps have smooth bodies and do not collect pollen.

HOME, SWEET HOME

You cannot escape bees and wasps unless you move to Antarctica! Both insects are found throughout the world, in nearly every **habitat**. Some bee and wasp species are solitary, or live alone. Solitary wasps may build small nests or live in holes in walls. Solitary bees most often make homes in small holes in the ground.

Wasps that chew up wood to make paper nests, as these ones are doing, are called paper wasps. Those that build nests from mud are sometimes called mud daubers.

A honeybee hive will have around 100,000 cells in it. These cells will hold around 15 pounds (7 kg) of honey and provide nursery space for some 20,000 eggs and larvae.

Once a wasp nest is complete, it might look like this one.

Some bee and wasp species are social, or live in groups. Many social wasps build nests using mud or by chewing up wood and plant parts to make a paper-like material. Social bees build hives in places like hollow tree trunks. They then start making combs out of beeswax, which is made in their own bodies!

BEE AND WASP LIFE CYCLES

Bees and wasps go through similar life cycles. The queen is the female that **mates** with male drones and lays eggs. **Fertilized** eggs will hatch as females, and eggs that are not fertilized will hatch as males. Workers are the female bees and wasps you see outside of the nest or hive.

These worker bees care for the larvae in the hive. Their bodies make matter called royal jelly to feed to the young. When it is time for a new queen, they will feed some larvae extra royal jelly to create new queens.

Here are the nursery cells in a wasps' nest. You can see that some of the cells have been covered over. Soon adult bees will come out.

They build the nest, gather food, and feed the young.

The young, or larvae, undergo changes before becoming adults. As the larva grows, worker bees feed it. Then the workers seal the larva into its cell with beeswax. Inside the cell, the larva forms a cocoon and transforms into a pupa. The pupa eventually changes into an adult bee and leaves the cell.

NOW YOU KNOW!

Although bees and wasps can cause painful stings, you can appreciate the ways they benefit people. They **pollinate** plants, which bring the flowers we enjoy and the fruits and vegetables we eat. Honeybees make the

Bees are helpful insects. Most bees are not interested in stinging people, they just want to drink nectar and collect pollen from flowers and plants.

honey we eat and the beeswax we use to make candles. Many wasps prey on other insects we consider pests. Bees and wasps are all around you, and now you know ways that you can tell them apart.

GLOSSARY

abdomen (AB-duh-mun) The large, back part of an insect's body.

aggressive (uh-GREH-siv) Ready to fight.

antennae (an-TEH-nee) Thin, rodlike feelers on the heads of certain animals.

compound eyes (KOM-pownd EYZ) The larger eyes of insects, which are made up of many simple eyes.

defense (dih-FENTS) Something a living thing does that helps keep it safe.

fertilized (FUR-tuh-lyzd) Put male cells inside an egg to make babies.

habitat (HA-buh-tat) The kind of land where animals or plants naturally live.

herbivores (ER-buh-vorz) Animals that eat only plants.

iridescent (ir-ih-DEH-sent) Having many colors that appear to move and change.

mates (MAYTS) Comes together to make babies.

pollinate (PAH-luh-nayt) To move pollen around to different plants, which helps them make seeds.

prey (PRAY) An animal that is hunted by another animal for food.

species (SPEE-sheez) One kind of living thing. All people are one species.

thorax (THOR-aks) The middle part of the body of an insect. The wings and legs come from the thorax.

venom (VEH-num) A poison passed by one animal into another through a bite or a sting.

INDEX

WEBSITES

Due to the changing nature of Internet links, PowerKids Press has developed an online list of websites related to the subject of this book. This site is updated regularly. Please use this link to access the list: www.powerkidslinks.com/hatd/bewa/